THE RICH MAN AND LAZARUS - THE JEWS AND JESUS

GARRY D. PIFER

Copyright © 2025 by Garry D. Pifer

All rights reserved in accordance with the U. S. Copyright Act of 1978, the scanning, uploading, and electronic sharing of any part of this book without the permission of the author is unlawful piracy and theft of the author's intellectual property. If you would like to use material from the book, prior written permission must be obtained by contacting the author

ISBN 979-8-9895556-6-6 (Paperback)
ISBN 979-8-9895556-5-9 (eBook)
Library of Congress Control Number: 2025909968

Unless otherwise noted, Scriptures are taken from the *King James Version of the Bible*, KJV.

Other Scripture quotations taken from the following:

Brenton Septuagint Translation, translator Lancelot Charles Lee Brenton (1807-1862). Originally published 1851. In public domain.

Young's Literal Translation, YLT, translation made by Robert Young (1822-1888), published in 1862. In public domain.

The Bible in Basic English, BBE, a translation of the Bible into basic English by Professor S. H. Hooke. The New Testament was released in 1941 and the Old Testament in 1949, In public domain.

Weymouth New Testament, 1903 and 1912, in the public domain.

The Holy Bible, New Living Translation, NLT, Copyright © 1996, 2004, 2015 by Tyndale House Foundation. Used by permission of Tyndale House Publishers, a division of Tyndale House Ministries, Carol Stream, IL 60188. All rights reserved.

Amplified Bible, Classic Edition (AMPC) first published 1965 Published by Lockman Foundation
P. O. Box 2279
La Habra, CA 90632-2279

Emphatic Diaglott in public domain. First published 1864. Translated by Benjamin Wilson.
Greek-English interlinear.

The Holy Bible, English Standard Version, ESV, © 2001 by Crossway Publishing, a publishing ministry of Good News Publishers
1300 Crescent Street
Wheaton, IL 60187

Contemporary English Version, CEV, published by American Bible Society
101 N. Independence Mall, East Fl. 8
Philadelphia, PA 19106-2155

Holman Christian Standard Version (HCSB) New Testament copyright © 1999, whole Bible copyright © 2004 Published by Holman Bible Publishers Nashville, TN

Definitions and comments marked as follows:

Strong's Exhaustive Concordance of the Bible by James Strong, Copyright © 2009 by Thomas Nelson, Nashville, TN.

Thayer's Greek-English Lexicon of the New Testament by Joseph Henry Thayer. Copyright © 1996 by Hendrickson Publishers, Peabody, MA.

Vine's Expository Dictionary of Biblical Words by editors W. E. Vine, Merrill F. Unger, William White Jr. Copyright © 1985 by Thomas Nelson, Inc., Publishers, Nashville, TN.

The Companion Bible, Dr. E. W. Bullinger 1906-1922, Kregel Publications
2450 Oak Industrial Dr. NE
Grand Rapids, MI 49505

Any Internet addresses (websites, blogs, emails, etc.) and telephone numbers in this book are offered as a resource. They are not intended in any way to be or imply an endorsement by the author, nor does the author vouch for the content of these sites and numbers for the life of this book.

Interior design: www.fiverr.com freelance services
Cover design: www.fiverr.com freelance services
Cover image: Licensed stock image, Adobe Stock
Proofreader/editor: Anna Hagen

Printed in the United States of America
Published at Edmonton, KY
gdpifer@scrtc.com

1 TIMOTHY 2:4

Who will have all men to be saved,
and to come unto the
knowledge of the truth.

2 PETER 3:9

The Lord is not slack concerning His promise,
as some men count slackness;
but is longsuffering to us-ward,
not willing that any should perish,
but that all should come to repentance.

DEDICATION

I have written a short dedication for each of the books I have written and published. I've dedicated a couple of them to my wife. One was dedicated to a cousin that assisted me by reviewing my manuscript and offering his critique. I directed some of the dedications to those who, by their comments, inspired me to embark on my study and to others who assisted in other ways. I want to dedicate this book to one who has been most helpful for quite a number of my books, my special proofreader and editor, Anna. Thank you for the hours you have spent helping me to root out so many misspelled words, incorrect grammar, unclear terminology, and a lot of other unnecessary and confusing words. Not only are you a great proofreader and editor, you are a wonderful daughter!

CONTENTS

Introduction   1

CHAPTER ONE
The Rich Man and Lazarus Story Is A Parable   3

CHAPTER TWO
Identities Revealed   7

CHAPTER THREE
Understanding Death   13

CHAPTER FOUR
Examining Luke 16:22   29

CHAPTER FIVE
Hell – Hades   33

CHAPTER SIX
Looking At Luke 16:23   41

CHAPTER SEVEN
Fire In the Bible   45

CHAPTER EIGHT
The Story Continues Luke 16:24   55

CHAPTER NINE
Abraham's Response Luke 16:25-31   69

CHAPTER TEN
The Conclusion 75

About The Author 79

Other Books By Garry D. Pifer 81

Introduction

Thirteen verses in Luke 16 (verses 19-31) are, in my personal opinion, the most horribly misunderstood and wrongfully explained of the entire New Testament. They are referred to as the story of Lazarus and the rich man. There is considerable debate as to whether these verses are a parable or a true, real-life account of two individuals. Although there are some differences in explanation, most believe and teach that these two people, a rich man and a beggar named Lazarus, both died. It is taught that Lazarus went to heaven and the rich man went to an ever burning hell, to be there for eternity. It is so very sad that this is widely taught and believed when the Bible does not teach this at all.

Numerous erroneous statements are made in the many articles and commentaries on these few verses. Here are three.

1. "The Bible is clear that every person who has lived will spend eternity in either heaven or hell."
2. "The transition to our eternal state takes place the moment we die."
3. "When believers die, they are immediately in the conscious fellowship and joys of heaven. When unbelievers die, they are just as immediately in the conscious pain, suffering, and torment of hell."

All of these statements are supposedly confirmed and taught through this story of the rich man and Lazarus.

In the following pages we will do a thorough and detailed verse by verse examination of this account, drawing upon the clear and specific words of the scriptures. We will NOT just assume that what has "always been taught" is correct. We will ignore the traditions of men. Relevant side studies will be done and included to support and substantiate the explanations made. The basis we work from is this, "If it is written it is settled." Too often people would rather take someone else's word rather than the Word itself.

Garry D. Pifer
March 2025

CHAPTER ONE
THE RICH MAN AND LAZARUS STORY IS A PARABLE

It has been taught by many that this story is a literal account told by Jesus and not a parable. Even back in the medieval church and the Reformation it was believed by some that it was an account of actual people rather than a parable. John Calvin, for example, thought this because the story has a named character (Lazarus) which he didn't see in other stories that were clearly parables. To insist that this is NOT a parable one must overlook several facts. Never do we find any accusation of the rich man being guilty of any sin. He is just pictured as being rich. IF this were a literal story, the logical implication would be that ALL rich are destined to be lost. The beggar being described as homeless and destitute would imply that all homeless and destitute people will be saved. Not one word is spoken of the individual's righteousness. I don't believe we have many who would believe all rich people are lost and all homeless will be saved.

In context, we see that Jesus began speaking (Luke 15, verses 1-3) to the Jewish religious leaders. Let us read what is written. Mark 4:34, "But without a parable spake he not unto them: and when they were alone, he expounded all things to his disciples." Matt. 13:34 also states the same thing, "All these things spake Jesus unto the multitudes in parables; and without a parable spake he not unto them." We are told that Jesus DID NOT speak to these individuals without using a parable. He would later explain the parables to His disciples. In Luke 15 and 16 we find 5 separate stories but all were introduced as "this parable," Luke 15:3. It appears that they were all parts of one parable He was giving. The rich man and Lazarus story is the 5th part of this parable.

We are not given the explanation of these stories that Jesus would have given to His disciples later. However, we have the benefit of Jesus' many statements and teachings recorded for us in the 4 gospel accounts. We have the additional material written by the apostles Paul, John, and James, plus, most importantly, we have the Holy Spirit, which Jesus said would guide us into all truth. We can understand. We will look at this one story here and, as we look at it, we will find that Jesus gave enough information that the Jewish leaders He was speaking to caught part of what He was saying.

LUKE 16:19-31

Let us read through the story found in Luke 16:19-31. We'll use the King James Version of the Bible, as most of us are familiar with the rendering.

19 There was a certain rich man, which was clothed in purple and fine linen, and fared sumptuously every day:

20 And there was a certain beggar named Lazarus, which was laid at his gate, full of sores,

21 And desiring to be fed with the crumbs which fell from the rich man's table: moreover the dogs came and licked his sores.

22 And it came to pass, that the beggar died, and was carried by the angels into Abraham's bosom: the rich man also died, and was buried;

23 And in hell he lift up his eyes, being in torments, and seeth Abraham afar off, and Lazarus in his bosom.

24 And he cried and said, Father Abraham, have mercy on me, and send Lazarus, that he may dip the tip of his finger in water, and cool my tongue; for I am tormented in this flame.

25 But Abraham said, Son, remember that thou in thy lifetime receivedst thy good things, and likewise Lazarus evil things: but now he is comforted, and thou art tormented.

26 And beside all this, between us and you there is a great gulf fixed: so that they which would pass from hence to you cannot; neither can they pass to us, that would come from thence.

27 Then he said, I pray thee therefore, father, that thou wouldest send him to my father's house:

28 For I have five brethren; that he may testify unto them, lest they also come into this place of torment.

29 Abraham saith unto him, They have Moses and the prophets; let them hear them.

30 And he said, Nay, father Abraham: but if one went unto them from the dead, they will repent.

31 And he said unto him, If they hear not Moses and the prophets, neither will they be persuaded, though one rose from the dead.

These 13 verses contain a great deal of information when we look at and examine what is given. In the next chapter we will begin to extract what is there. God tells us, Proverbs 25:2, "It is the glory of God to conceal a thing: but the honour of kings is to search out a matter." The following pages will hopefully be an honor to each of us as we search out what is concealed, not from us, but FOR us.

CHAPTER TWO
IDENTITIES REVEALED

IDENTITY OF THE RICH MAN

In verses 19 and 20 we are told of two individuals that this story revolves around. Let us look at what Jesus tells us and determine just who Jesus is speaking about. The first one mentioned in verse 19 is "a certain rich man." "There was a certain rich man, which was clothed in purple and fine linen, and fared sumptuously every day:" Here is what we know from what is written. This "certain" man was "rich." He was clothed in "purple and fine linen," and "fared sumptuously every day." A bit later in the story Jesus reveals a little more. Jumping ahead to verse 24 we find that this individual refers to Abraham as his father, "And he cried and said, Father Abraham." In verse 28 the rich man states that "I have five brethren;" I believe that even the Jewish religious leaders that Jesus was speaking to began to understand.

Both "purple" and "fine linen" symbolized royalty and wealth. Both were used in clothing royalty and the priests. The tribe of Judah was the royal tribe of Israel. Let us look at Genesis 49. Jacob was speaking to his 12 sons. In verse 10 he states, "The sceptre (which is a symbol of kingship) shall not part from Judah, nor a lawgiver from between his feet, until Shiloh come;" The Jewish people or tribe were well known for their wealth and love of money. A few verses earlier in chapter 16 of Luke Jesus took these individuals to task for their covetousness and attention to mammon, or wealth, (Verses 13-14). Lest we forget, it was Judah who suggested they sell Joseph to the merchants rather than killing him (Gen. 37:26-27). Israel as a whole, and specifically Judah, regarded Abraham as their father. Judah, one of the 12 sons of Jacob, had five blood brothers, all born to Jacob's wife Leah. Those brothers were Reuben, Simeon, Levi, Issachar, and Zebulun. (Gen. 35:23) The Jewish people viewed themselves as the "chosen people" and to some measure still held to the covenant made with Abraham and the one made at Sinai. In that regard they were "rich and fared sumptuously." Clearly the "rich man" symbolizes the Jewish nation, the people of Judah, the very Jewish leaders Jesus was speaking to.

LAZARUS IDENTIFIED

Now, let us turn to the second individual in this story, Luke 16: 20-21. "And there was a certain beggar named Lazarus, which was laid at his gate, full of sores, and desiring to be fed with the crumbs which fell from the rich man's table: moreover the dogs came and licked his sores." Many have taught that since this individual was given a name in the story it had to be a literal occurrence. No, it is just an important statement regarding this person, as names, especially in scripture, have meanings. When we examine the meaning of the name "Lazarus" we begin to get an inkling of his identity. Numerous internet sites provide the following information. "It appears pretty widely accepted that Lazarus is merely a Latinization of the Greek *Lazaros* which is a transliteration of the Hebrew name Eleazar (or Elasar or Eliezer)." This tells us where we get the name, but what does it mean? The name Eleazar is a compound of two elements. The first part is the Hebrew word *El*, the common abbreviation of *Elohim*, most often translated into English as "God." The second part of the word is the Hebrew verb *azar*, meaning "to help." The name Lazarus then means "God is help," "God of help," "God is my helper," "God will help." Jesus is plainly indicating that He, Jesus, is the Lazarus of the parable, He was God in the flesh who came bringing help to the Jews and all of mankind. This becomes even clearer as we continue.

Jesus tells us that Lazarus was a beggar. Why would He do that? He was describing this individual as the Jews viewed Him. They saw Jesus as a poor person born of common and poor parents. He didn't receive education at the feet of well known and respected "doctors of the law." He was brought up and trained in a trade, the son of a carpenter. He did not own great possessions and often in His traveling He "had no place to lay His head." Jesus was the Messiah that the Jews were looking for but they expected Him to come as a conquering king. They totally overlooked the prophecy given by Isaiah, recorded in Isa. 53:2-3, "...he hath no form nor comeliness; and when we shall see him, there is no beauty that we should desire him. He is despised and rejected of men; ...and we hid as it were our faces from him; he was despised, and we esteemed him not." The Jewish leaders totally failed to recognize the One they were looking for.

Jesus continued to draw their attention to Isaiah 53. He said, Luke 16:20, "And there was a certain beggar named Lazarus, which was laid at his gate, full of sores." The prophecy proclaimed that the Messiah would be "acquainted with grief (sickness)" and would bear "our griefs (sicknesses), and carried our sorrows (pains)" (Isa. 53:3-4). The prophecy made it clear that the Messiah, would come bringing healing, "and with his stripes we are healed" (Isa 53:5). The Jewish leaders saw the many miraculous acts of healing that Jesus performed but did not recognize Him as the One they were looking for. Matthew, in his gospel tells us that Jesus was fulfilling that prophecy from Isaiah, Matt. 8:16-17, "...and healed all that were sick: That it might be fulfilled which was spoken by Esaias the prophet, saying, Himself took our infirmities, and bare our sicknesses." In Luke 4:17-21 Jesus read from the book of Isaiah, specifically Isaiah 49:8-9, which also speaks of Him coming with healing, and told those there that all of these prophecies were fulfilled by Him.

Verse 21 of Luke 16 gives us more important details of the story. For the moment let us look at the last part of the verse, "moreover the dogs came and licked his sores." The term "dogs" was used by the Jewish people in speaking of the gentiles. It is interesting that Jesus also used this term when speaking to the Syrophencian woman, Mark 7:25-30. It's a basic instinct in dogs, and many other animals, to lick their own sores and wounds, as well as those of others. Jesus used this in His story, knowing as it has been discovered, that the animal licking the sore or wound soothes the pain, the saliva has antiseptic properties, and it cleans the sore. All of these things lead to healing. Jesus is indicating that some of the gentiles were coming to Him for healing. Thus, "the dogs," the gentiles, came and licked Lazarus' sores and received healing.

Let us look at the other items Jesus mentioned in Luke 16:20-21, "which was laid at his gate, full of sores, and desiring to be fed with the crumbs which fell from the rich man's table:" Jesus, Lazarus the beggar, it says, was laid at the gate, at the very door of the rich man, the Jewish people. This is very much like what Jesus stated in Revelation 3:20, "Behold, I stand at the door, and knock: if any man hear my voice, and open the door, I will come in to him, and will sup with him, and he with me." Jesus is stating in the parable that He, the Messiah, had come knocking, had come "unto his own, and his own received him not" (John 1:11). Jesus came with His message to His own, the Jewish people, but they didn't open to Him, did not receive Him. He desired even the few who clandestinely followed or believed on Him, the crumbs. We know of two, Nicodemus and Joseph of Arimathaea. Nicodemus came to Jesus at night, hidden by darkness from his contemporaries. It was only at the time of Jesus' death that he stepped out, helping to prepare Jesus' body for burial. John 19:38 tells us that Joseph of Arimathaea was a disciple, but secretly. There were, perhaps, a few others. These were the "crumbs."

With the identities of the two individuals of this parable established we are ready to begin our search for what has been concealed for us. Let us move on to Chapter Three.

CHAPTER THREE
Understanding Death

After identifying the two individuals, Jesus begins to tell the story in verse 22 of Luke 16. "And it came to pass, that the beggar died, and was carried by the angels into Abraham's bosom: the rich man also died, and was buried." So that we can properly understand what Jesus tells us we need to understand the things He mentions. Both died; one was buried and the other "carried by the angels into Abraham's bosom." Let us look to the scriptures to see what is "written and settled" by the Word. We'll look at what death is and what is written about it.

DEATH ACCORDING TO THE BIBLE

A quick Google search provides scores of definitions and ideas concerning death. Some ideas come are from a "scientific" point of view. Some thoughts come from political opinion. And, you will find many thoughts and opinions put forth by numerous Bible teachers and believers. Even those ideas vary. Here is a sampling:

"Death, dying, and the afterlife are all shrouded in deep mystery, cloaked in darkness and generally surrounded by fear and apprehension. The very idea of death strikes fear into many people's hearts."

"Death is the cessation of the connection between our mind and our body. Most people believe that death takes place when the heart stops beating; but this does not mean that the person has died, because his subtle mind may still remain in his body."

"Death may be the most misunderstood subject in the world today."

"Death, the total cessation of life processes that eventually occurs in all living organisms. The state of human death has always been obscured by mystery and superstition, and its precise definition remains controversial, differing according to culture and legal systems."

"Although there is no universally accepted definition of death, a 1971 Kansas statute comes close: 'A person will be considered medically and legally dead if, in the opinion of a physician, based on ordinary standard of medical practice, there is absence of spontaneous brain function.'"

Let us view a few thoughts and opinions from Bible teachers and believers.

"Death is inevitable to whatever is born. The Soul is free from the bondage of birth and death. It is eternal; it has no death. Anything that is born has to die, and because there is death, there will also be birth. So death is connected to birth. Wherever there is birth there is death."

"According to the Bible, death is not the end of life but the separation of the soul from the body. Scripture clearly speaks of both eternal life with God in heaven and eternal separation from God in hell."

"The Biblical definition of death - whether physical or spiritual - is not non-existence, but separation."

"Physical death is the separation of body and soul."

There is apparently no universal agreement on the subject of death. There are many opinions, beliefs and thoughts. But is there an authoritative source where we can get some answers? Yes, thankfully there is. We are going to see what the Bible says, what is written. We will look first at what Jesus taught. He was God in the flesh, by whom all things were created. He is the one who created and set in motion life and death. He knows whereof He speaks.

JESUS' TEACHING

We will begin by looking at His words in John 11 and 12. You are familiar with the story of Jesus' friend Lazarus (not the Lazarus of the parable) being raised from the dead by Jesus. There is SO-O-O much in this account and we won't attempt to cover all of what is there, but we will look at what Jesus has to say specifically about death.

Beginning in the first verse of chapter 11, John gives us a bit of the back story. Martha, Mary, and their brother Lazarus were friends of Jesus. John, in verse 2, recounts the event of Mary anointing the feet of Jesus with ointment and wiping His feet with her hair. John then gets right to the heart of the story by telling us that Lazarus was sick. This was a very serious illness, and the sisters sent a messenger to Jesus informing Him. All indications are that Jesus was at

Bethabara, beyond the Jordan, approximately 20 miles away from Bethany, perhaps a day's journey for the messenger. (See John 1:28 and John 10:40.)

In verse 4 we read Jesus' response, which was most likely carried back to Martha and Mary by the messenger. There has been much discussion over what Jesus said. Our English King James Version renders His words thus, "This sickness is not unto death, but for the glory of God, that the Son of God might be glorified thereby."

We have the benefit of the rest of the story that John gives us and can gain understanding. Those standing there at the time, including Jesus' disciples, missed what He was saying. He knew by the Holy Spirit, that at the moment He was speaking, Lazarus had already died. The text tells us that word came to Him of Lazarus' sickness which, as we mentioned above, it would have taken a day for the messenger to arrive. In verse 6 we are told that Jesus remained where He was for two days. After this He and His disciples made the trip to Bethany, a full day's journey. When they arrived, we are told in verse 17, He found that Lazarus "had lain in the grave four days already."

So, what was Jesus expressing in verse 4? What did He mean, "This sickness is not unto death," when He was aware that Lazarus was already in the grave? Knowing, as we do from John's account we could possibly state it more clearly. Jesus could have as well, but He wanted His words to be a bit cryptic, keeping the meaning hidden and concealed.

Maybe it will be a bit clearer if we word it differently. For example, "Death, resulting from this sickness, is not the last word!"

"Although this sickness may bring death, that is not the conclusion to this situation." "Lazarus' sickness will result in great glory to God. He may die but it won't hold him." "This sickness will not end in a death lasting until the great resurrection of all, but will be one to bring glory to God and to His Son."

After making this statement, John tells us a couple of things that are important to the story. He tells us in verse 5 that Jesus loved Martha, Mary and Lazarus. He had a very special connection with them. Now, John tells us that when Jesus got the message that Lazarus was sick, He didn't go rushing off to Bethany, BUT He "abode two days still in the same place where He was." Now, as we rehearsed above, Jesus was fully aware of the situation and knew what He was doing.

Then, in verse 7, Jesus said to His disciples, "Let us go into Judea again." He didn't make mention here of Lazarus. And His disciples responded, saying in essence, "What are you thinking? The Jews recently were seeking you to kill you, and you want to go back there?"

DEATH IS SLEEP

We won't try to go into His whole response, given in verses 9 and 10, but let us look at verse 11. Notice His words, "Our friend Lazarus sleepeth; but I go, that I may awake him out of sleep." When the disciples heard this they said, "Hey, if he is asleep he'll be fine." John then explains, verse 13. "Howbeit Jesus spake of his death: but they thought that He had spoken of taking rest in sleep." Then Jesus said unto them plainly, "Lazarus is dead." (verse 14)

Did we catch what Jesus says? He equates death with sleeping. And, this was not a new concept to those there with Him. In the Old Testament scriptures we find this expressed over and over. In fact we find an interesting expression, mentioned in connection with various individuals, "slept with his fathers." This expression is used over 35 times and is clearly speaking of death. Let us look at one account, 1 Kings 2:10, "So David slept with his fathers, and was buried in the city of David." One isn't buried if he is taking a rest. As we read earlier, when Jesus said He was going to awake Lazarus from sleep, His disciples thought He was referencing "taking of rest in sleep." Jesus had to make it quite clear that He was speaking of death, verse 14 of John 11, "Lazarus is dead."

Jesus says two things with the same meaning. "Lazarus sleepeth;..." and "Lazarus is dead." This study won't look into all the scientific research about sleep, but I believe we all know what sleep is. We sleep every night (or day), and though we may not know all that research goes into, we do know the basics. We sleep. We are unaware of anything happening around us. We are unaware of the passage of time. We look at a clock and mentally calculate "how long we slept." I'd like to quote from a short article I found on the internet concerning sleep.[1] "In other words, a sleeping person is unconscious to most things happening in the environment." A bit later in the same article, "a sleeping person can be aroused if the stimulus is strong enough." It is stated that not only man but reptiles, birds and mammals all sleep. And, quoting again, "That is, they become unconscious to their surroundings for periods of time."

---

[1] https://tinyurl.com/4p96p3x2

OLD TESTAMENT WRITERS

When we are asleep we are unaware of what is taking place around us. We are unconscious to what is happening. Jesus is affirming what was known and understood by the writers of the Old Testament and by those around Him at the time, sleep is a shadow of death. Solomon, the wisest man who ever lived, knew and understood sleep and death. Notice what he writes in Ecc. 9:5, "For the living know that they shall die: but the dead know not any thing,…" Just as in sleep, we are unconscious, not knowing anything that is happening around us. When we are dead, we do not know anything. David, Solomon's father, also knew this truth. In Psalms 146 and verse 4 he writes, "His breath goeth forth, he returneth to the earth; in that very day his thoughts perish."

Back a few pages we read another verse that David penned expressing much the same thing. Psa. 115:16, "The dead praise not the Lord, neither any that go down into silence." Earlier in the Psalms David makes another statement along the same line. Psa. 6 and verse 5 he is in context speaking to God and says, "For in death there is no remembrance of thee: in the grave who shall give thee thanks?" No, the dead have no memory, no thoughts, are not praising God and giving Him thanks. They are "asleep"!

Isaiah the prophet tells us the same things we read from Solomon and David. Notice Isa. 38:18-19, "For the grave cannot praise thee, death can not celebrate thee: they that go down into the pit cannot hope for thy truth. The living, the living, he shall praise thee, as I do this day:…" Plainly it is only the living that are able to praise God. The dead are asleep, unconscious, to any and everything.

They are not able to praise and celebrate God. Their thoughts have perished.

Job, who lived long before David, Solomon or Isaiah, understood about death. Let us look at what he expressed while he was going through his trial. In chapter 14 of Job we read, beginning with verse 10 and through verse 14. "But man dieth, and wasteth away: yea, man giveth up the ghost, and where is he? As the waters fail from the sea, and the flood decayeth and drieth up: So man lieth down, and riseth not: till the heavens be no more, they shall not awake, nor be raised out of their sleep. O that thou wouldest hide me in the grave, that thou wouldest keep me in secret, until thy wrath be past, that thou wouldest appoint me a set time, and remember me! If a man die, shall he live again? All the days of my appointed time will I wait, till my change come."

Did you notice that Job knew and understood that death was equated to being asleep. Look again at the words he used. "But man dieth, and wasteth away;" "So man lieth down, and riseth not:" "they shall not awake, nor be raised out of their sleep." "All the days of my appointed time will I wait, till my change come." Yes, he knew that in death he would be asleep awaiting a resurrection.

Daniel also speaks of death as sleep, Dan. 12:2. The prophet Jeremiah speaks in the 51st chapter of Jeremiah about those who sleep a perpetual sleep. Brown, Driver, Briggs Concordance gives as the first definition of the word perpetual, "long duration." But, all of these men of God also knew and spoke of a time of awakening from the sleep of death, of a resurrection.

RESURRECTION

The resurrection was paramount in Jesus' miracle and teaching about death and sleep in John 11. When Jesus spoke to Martha as He came into Bethany, He told her that her brother would "rise again," verse 23. Martha believed in the resurrection of the dead and responded that she knew that Lazarus would rise again at the last day, verse 24. But, Jesus made His point, verse 25, "I am the resurrection..." He knew what He was going to do in just a short time.

As I said earlier, there is so much in this account. Jesus taught about death, but, He also taught about resurrection. And, in all of this we also understand that He was showing that He would soon die, be put into the grave, and be resurrected. Let us notice again what He says about Lazarus.

In verse 39 of John 11 we find Jesus at the grave, and He speaks to Martha. Look at how this verse refers to her, "Martha, the sister of him that was dead." Lazarus was dead. He had earlier said that Lazarus was asleep. Verse 44, after Jesus called for Lazarus to come forth, we read that "he that was dead came forth,..." Continuing the story in chapter 12 we are told that six days before the passover Jesus came to Bethany "where Lazarus was which had been dead, whom he raised from the dead." The resurrection of Lazarus, the raising him from the dead was, as Jesus had said in verse 11 of chapter 11, the act of awakening him out of sleep.

We have read what was written, what Jesus said, and what many of the Old Testament prophets and writers wrote equating death with sleep. Let us now notice what is written and recorded by Paul and other New Testament writers.

Luke wrote both the gospel of Luke and the book of Acts. In chapter 13 of the book of Acts, verse 36, he speaks of King David. "For David, after he had served his own generation by the will of God fell on sleep, and was laid unto his fathers, and saw corruption." Slightly different wording but exactly what we read earlier, "David slept with his fathers and was buried…"

The apostle Paul gave us a great amount of teaching on death and the resurrection. We'll look at a few passages. In his discussion of eating of the bread and taking of the cup in 1 Cor. 11:30, he speaks of those who eat and drink without proper discernment of the Lord's body. "For this cause many are weak and sickly among you, and many sleep." His reference to sleep is indicating that many had died when they should have been receiving healing.

We'll turn to the 15th chapter of 1 Corinthians in a moment, to what is referred to as "the resurrection chapter" but let us first look at Paul's words in 1 Thes. 4. Beginning with verse 13, "But I would not have you to be ignorant, brethren, concerning them which are asleep,…" As we continue reading it becomes quite clear that he is speaking of those who have died, not just taking rest. Verse 14, "For if we believe that Jesus died and rose again, even them which sleep in Jesus…" Let us continue, verse 15, "…that we which are alive and remain unto the coming of the Lord shall not prevent them which are asleep." He repeatedly calls death sleep. Now, we come to verse 16 where Paul makes it very clear that the sleep he has been speaking of is death. "…and the dead in Christ shall rise first." (I didn't quote every word Paul wrote here as there would be a dozen studies or sermons generated.)

Now, to 1 Cor. 15. Once again, there is so much that could be covered, but we'll look specifically at his statements correlating sleep and death. He begins teaching about death and the resurrection in verse 12, speaking of Jesus rising from the dead. Let us drop down to verse 18, "Then they also which are fallen asleep in Christ…" Verse 20, "…and become the firstfruits of them that slept." We know that his references to sleep are equated to death, as he continues in the following verses. 21, "For since by man came death, by man came also the resurrection of the dead." 22, "For as in Adam all die,…" 26, "The last enemy that shall be destroyed is death."

Going down to verse 51, Paul tells us, "Behold, I shew you a mystery; We shall not all sleep, but we shall all be changed." 52, "and the dead shall be raised incorruptible, and we shall be changed." 55, "O death, where is thy sting? O grave, where is thy victory?"

From one end of the Bible to the other, the words and teachings of Jesus are repeated by the writers of scripture; death is over and over again referred to as sleep, an unconscious state, in which one is unaware of what is going on around him. Thoughts have perished. It is a period of awaiting being "awakened" at the resurrection.

I know that "religion," has told us much that is contrary to what we have been reading. I hear many, without Scriptural support, state that when a person dies he has "gone home," or has "gone to heaven," or is now "with Jesus." One individual that I have learned a lot from and come to appreciate recently made a statement on a live-streamed study, that David had gone to heaven and was with Jesus. I wanted to shout out through the internet, "That isn't what Scripture says!" Let us read what the Bible tells us about David. Acts 2:29, which is part of Peter's message on the Day of Pentecost, "Men and brethren, let me freely speak unto you of the patriarch David, that he is both dead and buried, and his sepulcher is with us unto this day." He says David is dead (asleep) and is buried. But, wait! Let us read further. Notice, please, verse 34, "For David is not ascended into the heavens:..." This is plain and tells us exactly what we have been reading. David, along with all who have died, fallen asleep, is sleeping in his grave awaiting the resurrection, waiting to be awakened.

SPIRIT, SOUL, AND BODY

I know some of you are thinking and saying, "But don't the soul and spirit leave and go to God?" We read some of Solomon's statements earlier concerning death, and he also makes a statement regarding this question. Ecc. 12:7, "Then shall the dust return to the earth as it was: and the spirit shall return unto God who gave it." Is he saying, as many teach, that the spirit goes to heaven and is dwelling with God and all the saved who have died? How does that fit with the numerous scriptures we have just read about "sleeping" in the graves until the resurrection? Let us look at something else that Solomon said, Ecc. 3:21. "Who knoweth the spirit of man that goeth upward, and the spirit of the beast that goeth downward to the earth?" A few other translations make this question a bit clearer. Let us look at a few. Bible in Basic English, "Who is certain that the spirit of the sons of men goes up to heaven...?" Contemporary English Version, "Who really knows if our spirits go up and the spirits of animals go down into the earth?" New Living Translation, "For who can prove that the human spirit goes up...?"

Solomon, who was the wisest man who ever lived because of God's great gift, understood that the breath and the spirit left the body at death, that it "returned to God," BUT he didn't know and he asked how any knew just where it went; did it go up to heaven? There is no revelation on that. We know that it goes to God for safekeeping until the resurrection.

One of the greatest revelations we have came from the Apostle Paul. It is recorded for us in 1 Thes. 5:23, "And the very God of peace sanctify you wholly; and I pray God your whole spirit and soul and body be preserved blameless unto the coming of our Lord Jesus Christ." Several translations make this a bit clearer by stating "your whole being–spirit, soul and body." Thayer's Greek Definitions defines the Greek word, *holokleros*, Strong's G3648, here translated 'whole,' as "complete in all its parts, in no part wanting or unsound, complete, entire, whole." Without all three components we are not a "whole being." Not a perfect analogy, but your car is not whole if you just have the body but no engine and transmission. You might have an engine and transmission, but without a body to put them into you don't have a car.

We can get a bit of the picture of what death is like, again, from the reference to sleep. When we are asleep, the body is in a bit of a slowed down, suspended state. The soul and spirit, where our thinking, our emotions, etc. are located, also are inactive. When we are sound asleep we are not thinking, planning, or expressing emotions. The instant we wake up we may immediately recall what we were thinking before we "fell asleep." Or if we were sad, happy, etc. our emotions come back immediately. But, during sleep, as during the time we are dead, there are no thoughts; we are not praising God or cursing anyone.

DEAD IN CHRIST

There are so many related studies that cry out to be done after reading many of these passages, but they don't fall under the scope of this study. Let's just look at a few more verses. We read much of what Paul wrote in 1 Cor. 15. Let us review a few things before we turn to our final verses. Paul stated in verse 22 that in Adam all die and even so, in like accord, in Christ shall all be made alive. Note, the dead aren't alive. In verse 23 he tells us that all will be made alive "in his own order." And he gives us a bit of that order, Christ the firstfruits, afterward they that are Christ's at his coming. Paul tells us plainly who these are over in 1 Thes. 4:14, "which sleep in Jesus." In verse 15 he refers to them as "them which are asleep." Verse 16 he again refers to the "dead in Christ" rising first.

Okay, let us turn to our final passage over in the book of Revelation. Let's read chapter 20 though we won't attempt to explain all that is there in this study. In verses 1-5 John speaks of the devil being bound and then of seeing thrones and those sitting on them being given judgment. The description is of those that were martyred, who hadn't come under the deception of the adversary. He tells us that these would live and reign with Christ a thousand years. And, in verse 5 we are told that the rest of the dead didn't live again until after the thousand years. Then he tells us what he has just written about is the first resurrection, the resurrection of those that Paul called the dead in Christ, those that "sleep in Jesus."

John, here in Revelation 20, tells us about those that are a part of the first resurrection, verse 6, and of the devil being loosed for a short period after the thousand years. Now, to the verses that are most pertinent to our study. Verse 11 speaks of a great white throne and then in verse 12 he sees "the dead, small and great, stand before God..." This, in light of verse 5, is the rest of the dead, those who were not the dead in Christ, those who did not sleep in Jesus. Note, he says they were the dead. Verse 13 says they were resurrected from the sea and "death and hell delivered up the dead." Verse 14 also speaks of "death and hell." There are all kinds of teachings about this, but simply put he is saying "those that are in the grave," be it a watery grave or anywhere they may have been buried.

Judgment, the casting of death and hell into the lake of fire, can be discussed later. But, the point for now is that all of these were dead, and they were raised to life to stand before God. They were resurrected, not at Jesus' return when the "dead in Christ," those that were "asleep in Jesus," were resurrected, but in their order, as John said, after the thousand years.

This was not "spirit and soul" coming from heaven to be put back into a body and then to enter a period of judgment. A common teaching presumes that there has been a judgment at death for them to have been "sent upward or downward." No, based on all the numerous Scriptures we have looked at, what was written, when they died they were asleep, unconscious awaiting this moment being described, being delivered from the sea and their graves. All the dead, not in Christ, small and great, young and old, from all time periods, each "in his own order" will awake from this sleep of death to stand before God.

Although there is so-o-o-o much more we could look at, I believe the scriptures we have looked at tell us plainly that death is pictured by sleep. It isn't something unfathomable, something all that difficult to understand. Sure, there are aspects we may not totally grasp but we don't have to be confused by the many and varied teachings given by religion.

We are now ready to understand Jesus' words in Luke 16:22. That awaits us in Chapter Four.

CHAPTER FOUR
Examining Luke 16:22

Knowing the identity of the key individuals and having a true understanding of death let us move on and understand what Jesus was saying to the Jewish leaders. Let us read once again verse 22 of Luke 16. Jesus says, "And it came to pass, that the beggar died, and was carried by the angels into Abraham's bosom: the rich man also died and was buried;" Almost all explanations of this verse have the beggar dying and immediately going to heaven, as that is what "Abraham's bosom" supposedly means. It is taught that Abraham was in heaven and received the beggar. Is this what Jesus was saying? Let us look at this verse noting what the rest of the Bible teaches.

ABRAHAM'S BOSOM

Is "Abraham's bosom" heaven? This is the only time this phrase is used in the Bible. It was a "Rabbinical Phrase," as understood by many commentators. The Jewish Encyclopedia states, "In Jewish writings (this phrase) is a term signifying the abode of bliss in the other world." However, the word "bosom" is used in a few different places to denote intimacy. One such place is John 1:18, "No man hath seen God at any time; the only begotten Son, which is in the bosom of the Father, he hath declared him." If we look at what the scriptures reveal we understand that Lazarus' dying and being "carried by the angels into Abraham's bosom" didn't happen at one time. There was much that had to take place between the two events, just as Jesus died, at the hands of the Jewish leaders, was buried, rose again after 3 days and 3 nights, spent 40 days with His apostles, and then was taken up to heaven (Acts 1:9). Abraham WAS NOT in heaven awaiting Him. A number of years after Jesus' ascension we are told in Hebrews 11, the faith chapter, that Abraham and the others listed had not received the promise, verse 39.

When will Abraham receive the promise? Paul and John reveal to us the resurrections, plural. The "first" resurrection spoken of is that of the "dead in Christ," which includes Abraham. This will occur at Jesus' return to earth, at which time He will set up the Kingdom of God, with Abraham, the father of the faithful, at His side. A number of Bible translations use the term "to Abraham's side" rather than "bosom." (Holman Christian Standard Bible, English Standard Version, New International Version, among others.)

CARRIED BY ANGELS

Another question we need to answer is when was Jesus "carried by the angels"? To answer this it helps to define "carried." Both Strong's and Thayer's give the meaning to be "bring, carry away." Mark 8:38 speaks of Jesus' coming "...when he cometh in the glory of his Father with the holy angels." When Jesus returns He will be escorted, brought, by the holy angels. At Jesus 2nd coming He will be "carried," brought, accompanied by the angels, to be met in the air by Abraham and all of the dead in Christ who will be resurrected at that time. We are told that "his feet shall stand in that day upon the mount of Olives," (Zech.14:4) and He will establish the Kingdom of God.

RICH MAN DIED

The last part of Luke 16:22 says, "the rich man also died and was buried." We won't spend a lot of time here discussing this as we devoted chapter three to the subject of what death is according to the Bible. Jesus simply states in this parable that "the rich man died and that he was buried." He was "asleep" awaiting a resurrection. This would obviously be a different resurrection than the one Abraham and the "dead in Christ" were in.

CHAPTER FIVE
HELL – HADES

As we continue our study of the parable of the rich man and Lazarus we come to verse 23 of Luke 16. This verse says, "And in hell he (the rich man) lift up his eyes, being in torments, and seeth Abraham afar off, and Lazarus in his bosom." Again, before we can begin to fully understand what Jesus is saying, we need to understand a few things. First of all, what is He saying about the rich man in "hell"? Let us look at that before we proceed further.

HADES USED AS EQUIVALENT TO *SHEOL*

When the Old Testament was first translated into Greek (the Septuagint), apparently the word *hades* was used as the equivalent to the Hebrew *sheol*. *Sheol* simply meant the grave, the pit, the unseen. Although *hades* may have originally carried that same meaning, by the time of the Old Testament translation into Greek the word had additional connotations added. The following is from the book **The Fire That Consumes** by Edward Fudge (American Christian Theologian, 7/13/44-11/25/17).[2]

---

[2] The Fire That Consumes [Houston: Providential Press, 1982], pg. 205

"In Greek mythology Hades was the god of the underworld, then the name of the nether world itself. Charon ferried the souls of the dead across the rivers Styx or Acheron into the abode, where the watchdog Cerberus guarded the gate so none might escape. The pagan myth contained all the elements for medieval eschatology: there as the pleasant Elyusium, the gloomy and miserable Tartarus, and even the Plains of Asphodel, where ghosts could wander who were suited for neither of the above. The word hades came into biblical usage when the Septuagint translators chose it to represent the Hebrew sheol, an Old Testament concept vastly different from the pagan Greek notions just outlined. Sheol, too, received all the dead…but the Old Testament has no specific division there involving either punishment or reward."

Long before Mr. Fudge wrote the words quoted above, J. W. Hanson, D. D. wrote the book **The Bible Hell**, in 1888.[3] I'd like to share with you a few comments he makes regarding hades. "The Hebrew Old Testament, some three hundred years before the Christian era, was translated into Greek, but of the sixty-four instances where Sheol occurs in the Hebrew, it is rendered Hadees in the Greek sixty times, so that either word is the equivalent of the other. But neither of these words is ever used in the Bible to signify punishment after death, nor should the word Hell ever be used as the rendering of Sheol or Hadees for neither word denotes post-mortem torment. According to the Old Testament the words Sheol, Hadees primarily signify only the place, or state of the dead. The character of those who departed thither did not affect their situation

---

[3] The Bible Hell can be found at http://www.tentmaker.org/books/The BibleHell.html

in Sheol, for all went into the same state. The word cannot be translated by the term Hell, for that would make Jacob expect to go to a place of torment, and prove that the Savior of the world, David, Jonah, etc., were once sufferers in the prison-house of the damned. In every instance in the Old Testament, the word grave might be substituted for the term hell, either in a literal or figurative sense. The word being a proper name should always have been left untranslated. Had it been carried into the Greek Septuagint, and thence into English, untranslated, Sheol, a world of misconception would have been avoided, for when it is rendered Hadees, all the materialism of the heathen mythology is suggested to the mind, and when rendered Hell, the medieval monstrosities of a Christianity corrupted by heathen adulterations is suggested."

Dr. Hanson tells us that *sheol* should never have been translated as *hades* but should have been left untranslated as it was a proper name. Dr. E. W. Bullinger in Appendix 131 of The Companion Bible states that the rendering of *sheol*, being a proper name, when translated, was always rendered "the grave." If "a" grave was being mentioned the Hebrew word *qeber* or *keber* would have been used. *Qeber* is used 67 times in the Old Testament and is translated as "a grave," "graves," "a sepulcher," "sepulcher," and "a buryingplace." In the 65 times *sheol* was used it was translated in the KJV and many other English language translations as "grave, pit, and graves" 34 times, always specified as "the" grave, "the" pit, or "the" graves. If "a" grave was being referred to it was never used with "the."

THE GREEK LANGUAGE

Most of us are familiar with the story of the Tower of Babel. God scattered the people and confused the languages. Various languages were developed over time. Some of the earliest we know about were the Sumerian, Babylonian, and Assyrian which have come down to us on Cuneiform from ancient Mesopotamia. The ancient Egyptian languages were recorded in Hieroglyphics. Filmmaker Timothy P. Mahoney searched for scientific evidence that Moses wrote the first books of the Bible. The compelling evidence of the development of the Hebrew language is presented in his film, Patterns of Evidence The Moses Controversy.[4] Hebrew was the language of the Old Testament, and it went through various stages of development. It was many years later that the Greek language was developed. There were many Greek city states, each with different dialects. Gradually a common standard, called Koine, meaning "common," developed. This language spread and became the most common language of the Eastern Mediterranean, primarily due to the conquests of Alexander the Great (333-323 BC). Koine Greek became the dominant language in politics, culture, and commerce in the whole Near East.

GREEK PHILOSOPHY

Not only the Greek language, but also the many beliefs and concepts of the Greek philosophers were exported to the whole area conquered by Alexander. There were many philosophers such as Socrates, Pythagoras, Heraclitus, and Homer, but the one who had the most influence on later Christian thought was Plato, a student

---

[4] https://www.patternsofevidence.com/moses/

of Socrates. He lived just prior to the time of Alexander, about 428-347 BC.

What are some of Plato's beliefs that found their way into Christianity? Here is a quotation from Gerhard Kittel's Theological Dictionary of the New Testament, Vol. VI, p. 568. "Plato introduced into Greek philosophy the belief of the immortality of the soul and its many [re]incarnations up to the goal of final purification. According to the myth ... the soul goes to the place of judgment after leaving the body. There the judges order the righteous ... to ascend to heaven. ... The idea gradually changes from a descent of the soul to the underworld, to an ascent of the soul into heaven. The descent becomes an ascent." Plato taught that souls lived in heaven before being born into this creation, and that they ascended back to heaven when they had sufficiently learned philosophy after a series of reincarnations. He taught that the destiny of the body was to decay into dust but the hope of the soul was to be released from the flesh, and to ascend into heaven as a pure spirit. The wicked were to descend to the underworld, designated by the Greek word *hades*. *Hades* took on more meaning than the unseen, the grave, or the pit. The hope of a resurrection was a totally foreign idea to Plato and the Greeks. Many writers share this in their articles and books.

Plato wrote ten books, known as the Republic. The concluding book was the Myth of Er. Myth, to the ancient Greeks was not as we view a myth. To them it was a true story, a story that unveils the true origin of the world and human beings. Here are a couple of quotations regarding this Myth of Er. The first one is from an article written by a psychiatrist and philosopher and found on the

Psychology Today website.[5] "Plato concluded the ten books of the *Republic* with the myth of Er, which greatly influenced the Western mind, down to our very idea of heaven and hell. Although Plato 'invented' the myth of Er, he did draw upon pre-existing elements of Greek and Egyptian mythology and cosmology." The second quotation is found in an article titled Plato's Myths found on the Stanford Encyclopedia of Philosophy website, written by Catalin Partenie, PHD. "There are many myths in Plato's dialogues: traditional myths, which he sometimes modifies, as well as myths that he invents, although many of these contain mythical elements from various traditions. Plato is both a myth teller and a myth maker."

From the above quotations (and many more that can be found on the internet) it becomes quite apparent that once Plato, and others, "invented" the belief in an immortal soul they had to "figure out" what became of it after the body died. A "myth," or story, developed as to the eventual ascension of the souls of the "good people" to heaven (see a further study of this in my book **Do Christians "Go To Heaven" When They Die?**) The souls of the bad or evil people were, according to these teachings, sent to the underworld, labeled as *hades*. These false beliefs, along with the additional definitions added to the Greek word *hades*, found their way into Christian beliefs and teachings. These beliefs continued to evolve over time. Immanuel Kant (1724-1804) is stated to be the central figure in modern philosophy. He concluded that the soul was not demonstrable through reason, but stated that the mind

---

[5] https://www.psychologytoday.com/us/blog/ataraxia/202406/platos-most-beautiful-myth-retold-and-interpreted

inevitably must reach the conclusion that the soul exists "because such a conclusion was necessary for the development of ethics and religion."

While much more could be looked at and presented, I believe this is adequate to show that what Jesus was presenting in Luke 16:23 was the rich man rising up from his grave, not being in the fiery "hell" portrayed by the common and widespread teaching of most of Christianity. Let us move on to the next chapter and look at what Jesus was truly saying.

CHAPTER SIX
Looking At Luke 16:23

Luke 16:23 in the King James Version of the Bible says, "And in hell he lift up his eyes, being in torments, and seeth Abraham afar off, and Lazarus in his bosom." Let us come to an understanding of what this verse is telling us.

"LIFT UP HIS EYES"

We covered in great detail the definition of the word *hades* and the additional and unscriptural meanings that were added to it. You will remember that originally it was used as a direct equivalent to the Hebrew word *sheol*. *Sheol* simply meant "the grave" or "the pit." Understanding this, and what death is, it is very clear that the "rich man" of the parable is resurrected, brought to life. And there he stands, right within the grave he has been "sleeping" in. He "lift up his eyes," looking around, trying to come to grips with what has happened. Having been dead, "asleep," he has no consciousness of the passage of time. He is unaware of all that has transpired.

We will go through the story looking at what is revealed through Jesus' words recorded in the gospel accounts and Paul and John's writings. We will find, rather than a depiction of an ever burning "hell" that has been taught by so many, some very good news.

As he begins to grasp what has just happened, it states that he is "in torments." Most of us have heard this explained that he is in the flames of an ever burning "hellfire." The word "torments" is translated from the Greek *basanos,* Strong's number G931. The word is defined as "a touchstone, which is used as a means of testing and proving." The rich man indicates he is going through a purifying fire (not a literal fire, as we will see in the next chapter). If we jump ahead to verses 24 and 25, it states that he was being "tormented." That word is from an entirely different Greek word, *odunao,* Strong's number G3600. It means "to be in anguish." The word is used 4 times in the New Testament, twice here translated "tormented." The other 2 times it is rendered "sorrowing." The rich man is suffering mental anguish and is sorrowing over his situation.

We have already discussed what "Abraham's bosom" is. As he sees them together he begins to grasp the fact that he missed the resurrection that occurred at Jesus' return. Where he is now would be the time John tells us about in Revelation chapter 20. After this first resurrection, in which Abraham will be raised, verse 5 says that the "rest of the dead" didn't live again until the thousand years were finished.

Once again we see referenced "Abraham's bosom" or "Lazarus in his bosom." Simply put, Abraham is standing beside Lazarus, Jesus. It says the rich man sees them "afar off." The Greek word this is translated from is *apo,* Strong's number G575. The basic meaning usually denotes a separation. It means "away, in various senses (of place, time, or relation)." As we will see there is a separation as to "place, time, and relation".

We will continue our study of this parable with verse 24 after we look at the "purifying fire" in the next chapter.

CHAPTER SEVEN
FIRE IN THE BIBLE

Few of us associate the word "fire" with the Creator Himself. We generally think of destruction such as Sodom and Gomorrah. However, the attributes of "light" and "heat" from fire speak more of the Creator and His goodness than of a destructive force against His enemies. The writers of the Bible employed the use of "fire" in many different ways. A study of these many ways can be extremely fascinating. We will refer to only a few here.

EXAMPLES OF "FIRE"

One of the first examples we find is in the covenant God made with Abraham in Genesis 15:17. The King James Version has a "smoking furnace," and a "burning lamp." Other translations have it as a "flaming torch" and a "blazing torch." God appeared to Moses in a burning bush. During the exodus from Egypt, God was in the pillar of fire. When the covenant was made with Israel at Mt. Sinai God came down in fire and smoke. Psalms 104:4 states that God's ministers are "a flaming fire." Even God's Holy Spirit is likened to fire. When it was first given on Pentecost we are told that it "appeared unto them cloven tongues like as of fire" (Acts 2:3).

LOOKING AT LITERAL FIRE

We most often think of fire as destroying things. We may say things like, "His home was destroyed by fire." We understand what is meant, but actually what has occurred is the components of the house have been changed. The various elements in the wood, for example, have changed forms. Let me try to make this simple. I burn firewood in my stove to heat our home. Combustion is the process by which the elements within the piece of firewood change form. When wood is burned, the heat causes the chemicals from which the wood is composed to vaporize, mixing with the oxygen in the air to form new chemicals, including water and the gas carbon dioxide. Minerals remain as ashes. What was formerly a tree is no longer in the form of a tree, but the substance thereof is simply CHANGED into a DIFFERENT FORM and exists in its new form. The change is not a physical change but a chemical change. Thus, to burn means to CHANGE.

Fire changes things. A major change a fire makes is that it PURIFIES. Most of us don't realize that many of our English words speak of this. The Greek word translated "fire" in the New Testament is *pur* (pronounced poor), Strong's Number G4442. This Greek word is the root of many of our English words: PURe, PURity, PURify, PURge, PURification. The basic thread is that of purifying. The Hebrew word for fire has much the same meaning. A prophetic passage we should look at is found in the book of Malachi, chapter 3: 1-3. "Behold, I will send my messenger, and he shall prepare the way for me: and the LORD, whom ye seek, shall suddenly come to his temple, even the messenger of the covenant, whom ye delight in: behold, he shall come, saith the LORD of hosts.

But who may abide the day of his coming? And who shall stand when he appeareth? For he is like a refiner's fire, and like fullers' soap: And he shall sit as a refiner and purifier of silver: and he shall purify the sons of Levi, and purge them as gold and silver, that they may offer unto the LORD an offering in righteousness."

Jesus also mentions in a few passages a fire that "never shall be quenched." Was He speaking of fire that would burn for all "eternity" and never stop burning? Let us look at what He was saying.

NEW TESTAMENT USAGE OF *GEHENNA*

The word *gehenna*, rendered most often "hell" in our English language bibles, occurs 12 times, 11 times in the gospels and once in the book of James. *Gehenna* is a transliteration of *Ge-Hinnom* in Hebrew, the Valley of Hinnom, a deep, narrow glen to the south of Jerusalem, where, after the introduction of the worship of the fire-gods by Ahaz, the idolatrous Jews sacrificed their children to Molech (2 Kings 23:10). At the time of Jesus it was a place where all kinds of refuse was burned, much like "city dumps" used to be here in the United States before laws were enacted that required everything to be covered with earth, known now as landfills.

The 11 times the word *Gehenna* is used in the gospels it was spoken by Jesus. We need to understand what He was saying. Was He speaking of a place of "eternal torment" of immortal souls? NO! An article by Kaufmann Kohler, says, "The belief that the soul continues its existence after the dissolution of the body is a matter of philosophical or theological speculation rather than of simple faith, and is accordingly nowhere expressly taught in Holy

Scripture."⁶ The doctrine of *Gehinnom* evolved within Judaism over time. At the time of Jesus, in the early 1st century, the basic idea was of "the place of spiritual punishment and/or purification for the wicked dead."⁷ Jesus used the same term Rabbinical Judaism was using, *Gehinnom*, using the physical fire and burning in the Valley of Hinnom, to speak of a spiritual process of purification. Much of what Jesus was teaching His disciples has been terribly misunderstood.

UNQUENCHABLE FIRE

The statement Jesus made about "fire that never shall be quenched" is a simple enough statement to understand if we don't twist what "quench" means. Originally the word meant "to extinguish fire." Today it has been expanded somewhat to include "putting an end to something" or "to satisfy". Jesus was saying this purifying fire, pictured by the fires burning in *Gehinnom,* would not be extinguished or put out by pouring water on the flames. However, this fire He was speaking of would quit burning when all the fuel was consumed. He was NOT indicating that it would burn for "eternity" as it has been falsely explained.

In making this statement Jesus was quoting from Isaiah 66:24, a verse that His disciples knew. So did most of the multitude that was hearing Him. This verse in Isaiah 66 also mentions "their worm shall not die" and Jesus quotes that as well (Mark 9:44, 46, and 48). What is that all about? Immortal worms?

---

[6] https://jewishencyclopedia.com/articles/8092-immortality-of-the-soul

[7] https://www.jewishboston.com/read/ive-always-read-that-jews-don't-believe-in-the-concept-of-hell-is-that-true/

THEIR WORM DIETH NOT

IF Jesus had been speaking of the "hell" most have been told about, we have a bit of a dilemma in understanding what kind of worms never die (Mark 9:44, 46, and 48). Are there "immortal" worms? Or, are there worms that can withstand the fire? What was He saying? A simple little bit of research answers those questions. Strong's definitions says, "a grub, maggot, or earth worm." Thayer's speaks of these worms as "worms, specifically that kind which preys upon dead bodies." Hopefully we begin to understand. Flies of various types lay their eggs in rotting flesh, discarded food scraps, and other types of refuse. The natural process is for the eggs to hatch into "maggots," sometimes referred to as worms. Depending on temperature and other conditions this takes only a few hours. Within just a few days the maggots metamorphosis into flies. They never die (at least naturally) but are simply the larva stage of flies. These maggots feed upon the material until they make this change. They never burn up in the fire but live in the refuse that would be on the outside edges of the "garbage dump."

THE LAKE OF FIRE

There are five verses found in the book of Revelation that speak of a "lake of fire." Most theologians and believers see this as being the same as the Jewish *Gehenna*. Let us take a brief look.

Rev. 19:20 "And the beast was taken, and with him the false prophet that wrought miracles before him, with which he deceived them that had received the mark of the beast, and them that worshipped his image. These both were cast alive into a lake of fire burning with brimstone."

Rev. 20:10 "And the devil that deceived them was cast into the lake of fire and brimstone, where the beast and false prophet are, and shall be tormented day and night for ever and ever."

Rev. 20:14 "And death and hell were cast into the lake of fire. This is the second death."

Rev. 20:15 "And whosoever was not written in the book of life was cast into the lake of fire."

Rev. 21:8 "But the fearful, and unbelieving, and the abominable, and murderers, and whoremongers, and sorcerers, and idolaters, and all liars, shall have their part in the lake which burneth with fire and brimstone: which is the second death."

One thing these verses have in common is that they are all from the book of Revelation. In listening to the numerous individuals who quote and teach from this book, one thing that becomes apparent is that many take some passages literally and other passages as merely symbolic. It seems that the individual chooses which way to take them based on their own personal view. However, if we turn to the very first verse of the book, we are <u>told</u> how to take these passages. Revelation 1:1, "The Revelation of Jesus Christ, which God gave unto him, to shew unto his servants things which must shortly come to pass; and he sent and **signified** it by his angel unto his servant John." Did you catch that? I emphasized the word "signified" by putting it in bold characters. What does the word mean? Look at the following.

Strong's definition says "to indicate." Vine's Dictionary of Biblical Words states under the definition for the Greek word *semaino,* Strong's number G4591, "Where perhaps the suggestion is that of expressing by signs." I especially like what Albert Barnes tells us in his commentary of this verse. "He indicated it by signs and symbols." He then continues, "It properly refers to some sign, signal, or token by which anything is made known, and is a word most happily chosen to denote the manner in which the events referred to were to be communicated to John, for nearly the whole book is made up of signs and symbols." We need to be very careful in attaching a literal meaning to verses that are using a symbol.

It should be clear to us that the "fire" being depicted is likened to literal fire but is of a spiritual nature. Remember we are looking at a sign or symbol. We just looked at the passage in Malachi which speaks of purifying and purging the sons of Levi. This is the "fire of God." Let us notice a few things that substantiate this. John the Baptist, speaking of Jesus in Luke 3:16, says, "He shall baptize you with the Holy Ghost and with fire." The word translated "and" is the Greek word *kai,* Strong's number G2532. It is most often translated "and," however other accurate translations are "also, even, indeed, but." It is translated "even" over 500 times in the New Testament. What John was stating is that the Holy Ghost, or Holy Spirit, is a spiritual fire.

Looking at the five verses which speak of the "lake of fire" we find three of them also include "brimstone." The Greek word is *theion,* Strong's number G2303. Strong's definition is "sulphur." Thayer's adds "divine incense." Vine's says "originally denoted 'fire from heaven.'" Charles Pridgeon (president and founder of the Pittsburgh Bible Institute, 1863-1932) comments about "brimstone" and refers to the Liddell and Scott Greek-English Lexicon, 1897

Edition.[8] He says, "The word *theion* translated 'brimstone' is exactly the same word *theion* which means 'divine.' Sulfur was sacred to the deity among the ancient Greeks; and was used to fumigate, to purify, and to cleanse and to consecrate to the deity;" He continues a bit further on, "The verb derived from *theion* is *theioo*, which means to hallow, to make divine, or to dedicate to a god." It is here that he refers to Liddell and Scott. Mr. Pridgeon then comments, "To any Greek, or to any trained in the Greek language, a 'lake of fire and brimstone' would mean a 'lake of divine purification.'"

The apostle Paul also speaks of this fire, the fire of God. We won't quote the entire passage but just a couple of verses from 1 Corinthians chapter 3. Speaking about our foundation being Jesus Christ, Paul speaks of men building with gold, silver, precious stones, wood, hay, and stubble. Let us pick up his words in verses 13-15. "Every man's work shall be made manifest: for the day shall declare it, because it shall be revealed by fire; and the fire shall try every man's work of what sort it is. If any man's work abide which he hath built thereupon, he shall receive a reward. If any man's work shall be burned, he shall suffer loss; but he himself shall be saved; yet so as by fire."

Can we understand what John is telling us in these five verses about "the lake of fire and brimstone"? Those individuals "cast" into the "lake" will have the purifying divine fire of God working upon them to burn up the **works** built with "wood, hay, and stubble." The "lake of fire" is not to burn up, nor destroy, nor torment these individuals for all eternity. "But wait" some of you

---

[8] Charles Pridgeon, Is Hell Eternal? Or Will God's Plan Fail? Chapter Eleven

may be saying. "Revelation 20:10 says, that they 'shall be tormented day and night for ever and ever'." Yes, that is what the King James Version says. Once again the translation is the issue. The Greek word translated "ever" (2 times) is *aion*, Strong's number G165. Strong's definition is "properly an age." Vine's also says "an age." Among a number that translate this passage as "ages of the ages" are Literal Translation of the Bible, Weymouth New Testament, and Young's Literal Translation. The time that this purifying takes may be quite some length of time, but it ends when the purifying has been accomplished by the action of the Divine Fire of God.

Verse 12 of Revelation 20 tells us of the dead, small and great, and the judgment that is to be upon them. As we continue reading we are told that "death and hell" delivered up the dead. "Hell" simply means the grave. Verse 14 has a statement that has been the basis of much doctrinal debate, "This is the second death." This phrase answers the first part of the verse, "And death and hell were cast into the lake of fire." When the work of the Divine Fire is done there will no longer be any death or any graves. Their ending is "the death of death." We were told in 1 Corinthians 15, the resurrection chapter, verse 26, "The last enemy that shall be destroyed is death."

I believe that with this understanding of fire in the Bible we can begin to grasp what the rich man in the parable is facing. Let us return to the story

CHAPTER EIGHT
THE STORY CONTINUES
LUKE 16:24

In verse 24 the rich man (the Jewish people, see Chapter Two), beginning to grasp the situation and remembering what Jesus had spoken when He addressed their attitude and their words, cries out for mercy and forgiveness. What were those words? In Matthew 12 and Mark 3 we read of the sin Jesus said they were guilty of, blasphemy of the Holy Spirit. This has been mistakenly called "the unpardonable sin." Before we continue here in Luke 16 with the story of the rich man and Lazarus, let us take a quick look at this sin and what Jesus said about it.

"THE UNPARDONABLE SIN"

Many have heard the frightening words of the evangelist that they could be guilty of a sin so great and so devastating in its awfulness that the shed blood of Jesus Christ could not wash it away, a sin that could never be forgiven, an unpardonable sin. They are told that the scriptures are there, that this sin does exist, and it is very possible they could sin such a horrendous sin. I ask, does such a sin exist, and if so, could you or I possibly have committed such a sin, or might we be in danger of committing it in the future?

MATTHEW 12:22-32

Most who teach that there is such a sin will turn to a teaching given by Jesus. This teaching is recorded for us in two of the gospel accounts. Sadly, most who teach this doctrine have not taken the time to really study these accounts and harmonize them with all scriptures. Let us turn to Matthew's gospel and read what is recorded for us, Matthew 12:22-32. Let us look at the context and look at what Jesus said regarding the subject. When we go to the first few verses of the chapter, we find that the Pharisees accused Jesus and His disciples of breaking the Sabbath by plucking a few heads of grain, rubbing out the kernels, and eating them. Following this encounter, Jesus and His disciples went into the synagogue, verse 9. We find that again the ones there asking questions to tempt Him were the Pharisees. After Jesus healed a man with a withered hand, the Pharisees went out and held a meeting, to discuss how they could destroy Jesus, verse 14.

In verse 15 we are told that the multitudes followed Jesus, and He healed them. Now we come to the part where this "unpardonable" sin is discussed. After Jesus healed an individual who was possessed with a demon, verse 22, we find that the people, the multitudes, recognized Him as the son of David, the Messiah. Guess who was on the scene speaking against Jesus? You guessed it, the Pharisees, the major religious group. Notice in verse 24 what they were saying, "This fellow doth not cast out devils, but by Beelzebub the prince of the devils."

If you call to mind some of the accounts we've been reading, you'll begin to notice that these guys had a perpetual fear that they might lose their hold on the people, and they were willing to do almost anything to keep the people from following Jesus. They were quite proud of their reputation. They knew that the people had been supporting their power and filling their purses. They believed that if Jesus' popularity and power continued to increase, they were going to lose everything they had. They had to admit that what had just taken place here, a demon possessed individual being healed of blindness and his inability to speak, involved something other than natural human power. Obviously they weren't going to admit that Jesus was doing this by the power of God. So what did they do? They accused Him of doing it by the power of the devil.

Let us notice Jesus' response, verses 25-28, from the Amplified Version. "And knowing their thoughts, He said to them, Any kingdom that is divided against itself is being brought to desolation and laid waste, and no city or house divided against itself will last or continue to stand. And if Satan drives out Satan, he has become divided against himself and disunified; how then will his kingdom last or continue to stand? And if I drive out the demons by the help of Beelzebub, by whose help do your sons (the exorcists of the Jews) drive them out? For this reason they shall be your judges. But if it is by the Spirit of God that I drive out the demons, then the kingdom of God has come upon you before you expected it."

Now we come to the closing words of the paragraph. Jesus addresses these words to these same self-righteous religious leaders of the Jewish nation. The solemn words that Jesus utters demand our attention. We need not place undue emphasis on them, but neither do we need to minimize what He says. If we aren't careful, we can read into these words meanings He never intended, or we can explain away these most solemn words. Let us read these words, verses 31-33, from the King James Version, "All manner of sin and blasphemy shall be forgiven unto men: but the blasphemy against the Holy Ghost shall not be forgiven unto men. And whosoever speaketh a word against the Son of man, it shall be forgiven him: but whosoever speaketh against the Holy Ghost, it shall not be forgiven him, neither in this world, neither in the world to come."

What is the sin against the Holy Spirit? We find the parallel account to what we have just read here in Matthew 12 over in Mark the third chapter, verses 22-30.

MARK 3:22-30

Let us look at verses 28-30 of Mark 3 in the King James Version. "Verily I say unto you, All sins shall be forgiven unto the sons of men, and blasphemies wherewith soever they shall blaspheme: But he that shall blaspheme against the Holy Ghost hath never forgiveness, but is in danger of eternal damnation. **Because they said, He hath an unclean spirit.**" (Emphasis mine.) We get a clue here. The opposition the Pharisees had toward Jesus wasn't just a spur of the moment thing. It is obvious that they knew what they were doing and saying. Remember the story of Nicodemus, a Pharisee who came to Jesus at night. He told Jesus, John 3:2, "Rabbi, we know that thou art a teacher come from God: for no man can do these miracles that thou doest, except God be with him." Many of these Pharisees, if not most, knew better but still plotted to destroy Jesus. Jesus presented a threat to their position and power over the people. Jesus warned them of the consequences of their attitude and actions. Their sin was not against God in heaven or the Son of God on earth.

They were resisting, opposing, and attacking the Holy Spirit, the very activity and administration of God toward them. Jesus warned them that they were in danger of blaspheming the Holy Spirit.

We often think of the Holy Spirit as "power," and certainly there is power, but perhaps it might be better viewed here as "force," God's energy force, by which He accomplishes His purpose and executes His will. As we look at what was going on, we see that these religious leaders were not in danger of committing this sin because they said Jesus was performing His miracles by the power of the devil. Jesus said that could be forgiven. They were expressing an attitude of unbelief which was a calculated rejection of the activity of God toward them. They were resisting the Holy Spirit. Notice what Stephen said to these same Pharisees right before he was stoned. Acts 7:51, "Ye stiffnecked and uncircumcised in heart and ears, ye do always resist the Holy Ghost."

As we just saw in these passages, Jesus was not addressing His disciples nor the people who came to hear Him and to receive healing. He was speaking directly to the Pharisees, the leaders of the Jewish nation. Jesus stated that He came to His own, His own people and nation, and "his own received him not" (John 1:11). His statements were directed at the Jewish nation, specifically the religious leaders. He was not directing His words to you and me. Blasphemy against the Holy Spirit was serious. It was greater than speaking against the Father or the Son. These same people, the leaders, were the ones who trumped up the charges against Him and had Him crucified. But, for all of that they were forgiven. Luke 23:34 records for us Jesus' prayer to the Father, "Father, forgive them; for they know not what they do."

Let us read again His statement in Matthew 12:31, "All manner of sin and blasphemy shall be forgiven unto men." Jesus says ALL. The Greek word is *pas*, Strong's number G3956. It is defined as a primary word meaning "all, any, every, the whole, each, everyone, all things, everything." Of the 1238 times this word is used, it is translated "all" 975 times. It means ALL. It means that there IS NO UNPARDONABLE SIN. So, how do we reconcile the rest of the verse?

Let us read again what Jesus said, "but the blasphemy against the Holy Ghost shall not be forgiven unto men" (Matt. 12:32). Let's not stop here. In verse 32 Jesus says, "it shall not be forgiven him, neither in this world, neither in the world to come." Jesus adds some additional information here. He says the forgiveness to men is "not" in "this world" or in "the world to come." What is He saying?

NEITHER IN THIS WORLD, NEITHER IN THE WORLD TO COME

The King James Version of the Bible we have been quoting says "neither in this world, neither in the world to come." However, that isn't quite the meaning of the Greek. The Greek word that is translated here as "world" is *aion*, Strong's number G165. The definition is "properly an age." The duration of an "age" is indefinite but does have an ending. If the translators had used the correct word "age" instead of "world" much confusion could have been avoided. Several other translations have corrected this. Here are a few: "Whoever may speak against the Holy Spirit, it shall not be forgiven him, neither in this age, nor in that which is coming." (Young's Literal Translation) The Weymouth New Testament renders this as, "Whoever speaks against the Holy Spirit shall obtain forgiveness neither in this age or in the age to come." One of the most popular translations, The New International Version, renders it, "Anyone who speaks against the Holy Spirit will not be forgiven either in this age or in the age to come." The English Standard Versions says, "but whoever speaks against the Holy Spirit will not be forgiven, either in this age or in the age to come." Jesus was plainly telling these individuals that forgiveness would not come in the age they were living in, nor would it come in the next age. Based on His statement that all sin shall be forgiven, He was warning that forgiveness would come, but not until a following age. (Note: We can assume Jesus was speaking of the age of Law, this age, and the church age, the age to come. Nowhere are we told how many ages there may be, when they begin, nor when they end.)

If we are honest with the scripture, we can plainly see that Jesus' words do not prove nor proclaim that there is an unpardonable sin. First, He says ALL MANNER of sin and blasphemy shall be forgiven unto men. Secondly, He states that some sins could be forgiven in the age they were living in. He then states, thirdly, that other sins against the Holy Spirit could not be forgiven in the age when Jesus came to earth, nor in the age to immediately follow. These words clearly indicate that sins not forgiven in those two ages will be forgiven in an age to come. There is absolutely nothing about a sin that is "unpardonable" throughout endless ages to come.

Let us go one more time to Mark 3. Verse 29 says, "But he that shall blaspheme against the Holy Ghost hath never forgiveness, but is in danger of eternal damnation." The concluding phrase, "but is in danger of eternal damnation," needs to be looked at briefly.

Several things again bring confusion. The word "eternal" is most often believed to be "never ending" or "without end." It is from the Greek word *aionios*, Strong's number G166. It, as you can probably see by looking at the word, is derived from *aion* which we just looked at. It means "age during" or "age lasting." A correct rendering of "damnation" would be "judgment." This verse from the original should be rendered "has not for the eon (age) forgiveness, but is in danger of eonian (age-during) judgment." This gives a much different meaning. The Emphatic Diaglott has it, "But whoever may blaspheme against the Holy Spirit, has no forgiveness to the age, but is exposed to Aionian Judgment."

Jesus was telling these leaders of the Jewish people that they would not, as a nation, receive His salvation until after that age and the then coming age were past. Paul tells us that "all Israel shall be saved," Romans 11:26. But, he said just prior to those words, verse 25, that it wouldn't be "until the fulness of the Gentiles be come in." He was aware of Jesus' statement that it would be after the two ages He addressed. Perhaps his statement helps us understand the statement that "the last shall be first and the first last" (Matt. 20:16). Israel, the Jewish people, were the chosen, the ones Jesus came to, the ones who were to be first. In their rejection the Gentiles, who would have been last, became the first.

Once we look at what Jesus actually said, we can rejoice that there is no sin that won't be forgiven. There is no sin that God the Father and Jesus won't forgive, no sin that Jesus' blood doesn't cover. Let us return to verse 24 of Luke 16, where the rich man is raised up following the age he had lived in, following the "church age," and the millennium.

"IN THIS FLAME"

The rich man, depicting the Jewish people, cries out for mercy, for forgiveness. Notice his request, (verse 24) "and send Lazarus, that he may dip the tip of his finger in water, and cool my tongue; for I am tormented in this flame." Before we discuss the dipping of the finger in water and cooling the tongue let us understand what is meant by "this flame." The common teaching is that the individual is standing with the fires of "hell" licking at his legs and body. THAT IS NOT WHAT IS BEING SAID! Notice with me, please, that it DOES NOT say flames, plural. It says "this flame," singular. The Greek word translated into English as "flame" is *phlox*, Strong's number G5395. This Greek word is used 7 times in the New Testament and is translated "flame" each time. However, on all occasions but one it is linked with the Greek word *pur*, Strong's number G4442, which is translated "fire" in English. 5 times it is rendered "flames of fire" and once as "flaming fire," The one and only time *phlox* is NOT connected to *pur* is here in Luke 16:24. This word, without *pur*, has an entirely different meaning. Notice what Vine's Expository Dictionary of New Testament Words has to say: "*phlox* 5395, akin to Lat. *fulgeo*, 'to shine,' is used apart from *pur*, 'fire,' in Luke 16:24; with *pur*, it signifies 'a fiery flame,' lit., 'a flame of fire.'" The literal meaning of the word used here, therefore, is "to shine." Only when used with fire (*pur*) does it have the significance of fiery flames. The Latin *fulgeo* is defined, "to shine, flash, glow, gleam, glitter, shine forth, be bright." Noting the relationship with the Latin *fulgeo*, "flame" would be best translated into English as "bright, radiant shining."

Let us grasp what is being said here. Instead of referring to intense heat and the "flames of fire" the "flame" is speaking of a very bright light. What would that symbolize? 1 John 1:5 states that God IS light. In his gospel account John states that Jesus was the light come from God. Notice John 1:6-9, "there was a man sent from God, whose name was John (John the baptist). The same came for a witness, to bear witness of the Light, that all men through him might believe. He (John) was not that Light, but was sent to bear witness of that Light. That was the true Light, which lighteth every man that cometh into the world." Jesus was THE Light. He "lighteth every man," every individual ever born, to reveal Himself and His goodness to all. Here in the parable we find that light coming upon the rich man, the Jewish people, at the time of their resurrection. This intense light shining upon them works to purify them, the purifying fire of God, the lake of fire we discussed earlier.

Just a few short years after Jesus spoke this parable we see this literally happening, a brilliant light coming upon an individual. Yes, I'm speaking of Saul, who became the apostle Paul. This is such a significant occurrence we read of it more than once. Saul was very much like the rich man of the parable. He was an individual of some means, having dual citizenship, being schooled at the feet of the most prominent Jewish doctor of the law, a pharisee of the pharisees. He had a hatred of those who were adhering to and following the teachings of Jesus and His apostles. God used "light" to deal with him. Luke gives us the account in Acts 9. Verse 3 says that as Saul came near Damascus "suddenly there shined round about him a light from heaven." Paul recounts this event for us. He says, Acts 22:6, "suddenly there shone from heaven a great light round about me." He mentions the light again in verse 9. In verse 11 he says that he "could not see for the glory of that light." Some translations of this verse, instead of glory, use the words "bright," or "brightness." The Weymouth translation says "so dazzling." Paul tells us, as recorded in Acts 26:13, "I saw in the way a light from heaven, above the brightness of the sun, shining round about me and them which jouneyed with me."

This intense, bright, dazzling light which Paul experienced is the same "flame" the rich man in the parable was experiencing, the purifying fire of God. Paul was blinded by the "light," but had his eyes opened to see Jesus. It has been stated by many Bible teachers and preachers that God won't "violate your will." He doesn't have to. He can bring things to bear that the individual will of his own accord change his will. Notice that Saul wasn't "forced" but through this purifying fire he voluntarily changed his will. He was brought to see Jesus as Lord and surrendered to Him. So, the rich man, the Jewish people, also will be brought to see God and His Son and receive their salvation, the forgiveness of all sins, including the blasphemy of the Holy Spirit.

"DIP THE TIP OF HIS FINGER IN WATER, AND COOL MY TONGUE"

There is much to look at and understand in these 12 words of Luke 16:24. IF the rich man of the parable had been in the "flames of an ever burning hell," as is generally taught, a small amount of water on a finger would do little to alleviate the situation. And, why was the individual concerned about his tongue? What does it mean to "cool" the tongue? Let us begin to look at and understand what this all means.

We discussed earlier the words of Jesus to the Jewish people, that they were guilty of "blasphemy of the Holy Spirit." There were many other words they had used against Jesus. They accused Him of being a sinner, being a glutton and a winebibber. They called Him a Samaritan, said He had a demon and was casting out demons by Beelzebub, and many other things. The rich man of the parable was beginning to see that his tongue had been used to voice all of these things. He was seeing the things about the tongue that James would write about in his epistle, "the tongue is a fire, a world of iniquity." (see the whole section, James 3:5-10) The Jewish people knew the many scriptures which spoke of the proper use of our words. Even the Sages of the Jewish religion considered "evil speech" to be one of the worst sins of all. According to the sages, "there are three transgressions for which a person is punished in this world and has no share in the world to come – idolatry, illicit sex, and bloodshed – and evil speech is as bad as all three combined."

The rich man, the Jewish people, were very familiar with and knowledgeable of the numerous rituals of the ancient tabernacle/temple. Water was used in many of the purification rituals. It was seen as wiping impurities clean. Let us notice one verse from the book of Numbers. It was part of God's instruction to Moses regarding the Levites, Numbers 8:7. "And thus shalt thou do unto them, to cleanse them: sprinkle water of purifying upon them." Water was an agent of purification and cleansing. The spiritual application is seen in Paul's words to the church at Ephesus and to us, Eph. 5:25. He is speaking of Jesus and the church. "That he might sanctify and cleanse it with the washing of water by the word."

The rich man was seeking a cleansing, a purifying, of his tongue, which he had used so improperly and evilly. He was seeking Lazarus', Jesus', forgiveness and cleansing. He was asking for just a touch of the finger which had been dipped in the water. This was to him a ritual of purification. He felt it would "cool his tongue." Exactly what was that all about? The Greek word translated "cool" is *katapsucho,* Strong's number G2711. Its meaning is "to cool down" or "to refresh." It is used to describe the act of cooling or refreshing something. It implies a restoration or renewal.

The rich man, the Jewish people, were familiar with the Greek translation of the Old Testament, the Septuagint. Gen. 18:4 uses this Greek *katapsucho.* Brenton's, the English translation of the Septuagint, renders it as "refresh." The King James uses the word "rest." The connection of the verse is with water. "Let a little water, I pray you, be fetched, and wash your feet, and **rest** yourselves under the tree." Obviously, in this parable, we find the rich man, the Jewish people, wanting the tongue cleansed, purified, and refreshed.

We will pick up the story the parable is telling us continuing in verse 25 of Luke 16 in the next chapter. We will look at Abraham's response to the rich man's request.

CHAPTER NINE
Abraham's Response
Luke 16:25-31

Verses 25 and 26 of Luke 16 contain Abraham's response to the rich man's request for mercy and for him to send Lazarus to touch his tongue with a finger dipped into water. Let us read these verses again.

"25 But Abraham said, Son, remember that thou in thy lifetime receivedst thy good things, and likewise Lazarus evil things: but now he is comforted, and thou art tormented.

26 And beside all this, between us and you there is a great gulf fixed: so that they which would pass from hence to you cannot; neither can they pass to us, that would come from thence."

"A GREAT GULF"

The timing here is at the resurrection of the rich man, the Jewish people, which will occur after the 1000 years following Jesus' return to earth from heaven. This is after the resurrection of Abraham and those that were the "dead in Christ." Abraham's instruction to the rich man is to look back and remember what had taken place during his lifetime. That lifetime would have been well over 3000 years earlier. He is told to remember the situation, the same information we were given in verses 19 and 20. The rich man, the Jewish people, had been blessed with "good things," the purple and fine linen. He, they, had "fared sumptuously every day." He was told to remember how Lazarus, Jesus, had been dealt with, had received "evil things." Notice, he was told, the contrast between the way things were in life compared to his present state of torment and Lazarus' glorious state.

Verse 26 begins, "And beside all this." Most translations have "besides," with an "s." A few others have "in addition," "moreover," and "yet." The Greek word translated "beside" is *epi*, Strong's number G1909. It is a preposition that is used over 800 times in the New Testament and is rendered into English about 40 different ways. The Greek word *epi* "is versatile and context-dependent" (Strong's lexicon). When used, as here, "with the idea of time, it looks backward and upward" (Companion Bible Appendix 104). There is an emphasis here of the time that had passed between the rich man's lifetime and the point where he has been resurrected. "Time" is key here. Jesus continued His parable, verse 26, with the word "between." Let us look at that word briefly.

"Between" is translated from the Greek word *metaxu*, Strong's number G3342. Strong's definition is "betwixt (of time) as adjective, intervening." Thayer's defines the word as "meanwhile, in the mean time." In these two verses, 25 and 26, we find several words relative to "time," lifetime, now, beside, between. "Time" is a difficult word to define. Merriam-Webster's dictionary says it is "the measured or measurable period during which an action, process, or condition exists or continues." Physicists define time as "the progression of events from the past to the present into the future." What is NOT mentioned in the various definitions given is that time ONLY applies to the PHYSICAL creation. Spirit is "outside of time." God, being spirit, is always in the NOW. God, Jesus, revealed Himself to Moses, and later to those He addressed while He was on the earth in human form, as I Am (Ex. 3:14, John 8:58, plus other verses). He DID NOT say "I WAS," nor "I WILL BE." He was always in the now, the present. (I know the Bible says He "is the same yesterday, today, and forever." We as physical humans relate to time past, time present, and time future. However, Jesus IS, the I AM.)

In verse 26 of Luke 16, after the word "between" is the statement regarding "a great gulf." Before we consider that let us notice the usage of a couple of words seldom used in our modern vocabulary, "hence" and "thence." Checking Webster's dictionary we find among the definitions the following. Hence, "from this time, after now." Thence, "from that time, thenceforth." "Time" is still the main item of discussion. The "great gulf," or *chasma* from the Greek (Strong's number G5490), is used just this one time in the New Testament. It is defined as "a chasm," "gaping opening," and was even a medical term for an open wound. However, here in Luke 16:26, as pointed out by some scholars, it indicates "an interval," and "is more of a dimensional aspect opposed to a physical aspect." The "great gulf" appears to be a time driven dimension of the physical versus the spiritual dimension of no time, always "the now." Abraham and Lazarus, Jesus, were in "the now." There was no going back 3000 plus years. Of course, those living 3000 years earlier could not be brought to the "now" in which Abraham and Lazarus were.

THE RICH MAN'S BROTHERS

Let us turn our attention to the remaining verses in this parable, verses 27-31.

27 Then he said, I pray thee therefore, father, that thou wouldest send him to my father's house:

28 For I have five brethren; that he may testify unto them, lest they also come into this place of torment.

29 Abraham saith unto him, They have Moses and the prophets; let them hear them.

30 And he said, Nay, father Abraham: but if one went unto them from the dead, they will repent.

31 And he said unto him, If they hear not Moses and the prophets, neither will they be persuaded, though one rose from the dead.

The rich man of the parable is still remembering his lifetime (verse 25) and "knows" that his brothers, the other tribes of Israel, were also not recognizing the Messiah when He came. His desire is that they could avoid the circumstance he is going through, facing the "flame," the dazzling light of purification the Bible refers to as "the lake of fire." He asks father Abraham to send Lazarus, Jesus, to them to testify, or as Thayer's says, "cause it to be believed." He wishes them to see and understand. The response from Abraham is that they had, just as he also had in his lifetime, Moses and the prophets. Recognizing himself and his own attitude in them, he tells Abraham that wouldn't be enough. He states that IF Lazarus, Jesus, who had been resurrected from the dead would go then they would respond. Abraham says that if they wouldn't hear Moses and the prophets, neither would they hear Jesus. It isn't stated here but you can imagine that Abraham reminded him, them, that Jesus was resurrected and all Jerusalem was discussing it without him, them, believing and changing.

CHAPTER TEN
THE CONCLUSION

Jesus ends His parable at verse 31 of Luke 16. He doesn't give a conclusion to all He has stated in these 13 verses. However, we can draw from what Paul and John recorded for us and know the conclusion. Let us look at what we are told. Romans 11:26, "And so all Israel shall be saved:" That is good news. How will that work? Paul tells us in 1 Corinthians 15:22, "For as in Adam all die, even so in Christ shall all be made alive." ALL will be resurrected. We looked at Revelation 20 earlier where we are told that those not in the resurrection of the "dead in Christ" at His coming "lived not again until the thousand years were finished," verse 5. Verse 12 speaks then of that time when "the dead, small and great, stand before God." People most often, when thinking of the resurrection, picture all the billions that have ever lived coming up at once. That is not the case. Even in the parable we have been looking at we see Judah raised but not his brothers. Paul explains this. We read verse 22 of 1 Cor. 15 a moment ago. Let us keep reading, verse 23, "But every man in his own order." He speaks of Christ's resurrection, then he says "afterwards they that are Christ's at His coming." The next words, verse 24, say "then cometh the end." There is much to transpire between the resurrection of the dead in Christ and the "end." ALL the rest of the dead will be raised and will be purified and reconciled, each in his own order. Paul says in verse 24 that, when the end has come, "Jesus shall have put down all rule and authority and power." That is of course ALL opposing rule, authority, and power. Note, the verse specifically states that there is a passage of time "till He hath put all enemies under His feet." Verse 26 tells us "the last that shall be destroyed is death." How is death destroyed? Everyone is made alive!

The parable of the rich man and Lazarus IS NOT about an "ever burning" hell fire, pictured by most Christians, and the contrast of a few in heaven. It truly is the GOOD NEWS of God's plan to bring all to reconciliation and salvation. Many, if not most, appear not to believe the beautiful words given us by Peter. Read and grasp these words found in 2 Peter 3:9. "The Lord is not slack concerning his promise, as some men count slackness; but is longsuffering to usward, **not willing that any should perish, but that ALL should come to repentance**." (Emphasis mine) No one can thwart God's will!

The parable given by Jesus does a number of things. It points out that the Jewish people refused to accept Him, refused to even truly recognize Him. He emphasized that although they could have been and should have been the first ones to receive forgiveness of their sins and salvation, they wouldn't obtain that position due to their sin of blasphemy of the Holy Spirit. The extremely GOOD NEWS was that there is an age to come when they will be dealt with, when they will endure the purifying fire of God, an age or time when the small and great will be raised. Most, it seems, believe that if one doesn't accept Jesus in this lifetime they are eternally lost and will endure the flames of "hell fire" forever. That is the worst false teaching foisted upon the world by the adversary. God is love! It is His will, His desire, that none should perish, **but that ALL should come to repentance!** His "purifying fire," the "God Fire," will bring ALL to see God's love, desire Him, and repent of their sins. ALL will be reconciled to Him and receive salvation.

About The Author

Garry D. Pifer has been a reader and student of the Bible for over sixty years. In the mid-nineties he embarked on a much more diligent study. He wrote most of his studies in article form, many being put onto the internet and some published in an independent journal. In 2020 he authored **God's Bestseller: Make It Real In Your Life!** This book is a handbook giving a step by step guide to studying the Bible, giving the reader the benefit of what he had learned over 25 years. Led by the Holy Spirit he has donated over 2400 copies to prisons and jails across America.

Garry and his wife, Connie, have been married for sixty years. They are the parents of four grown children. They have eleven grandchildren and six great-grandchildren. They currently reside in South-Central Kentucky.

Garry may be contacted by writing to him at P. O. Box 131, Edmonton, KY 42129 or by E-mail: gdpifer@scrtc.com

Other Books By Garry D. Pifer

God's Bestseller: Make It Real in Your Life!

Many have often wanted to understand the Bible but just thought it was a very confusing and closed book. In this conversational and straightforward book, Garry D. Pifer presents a step by step guide that will take you from a lack of understanding and a place of confusion to an opening up of what God has hidden FOR you, not from you. This book will give you direction in your search of the Scriptures. You will find priceless riches and treasures of great price. Read this book and learn how to find what has been concealed.

Shadows of Jesus in the Exodus

Most have not grasped the numerous shadows in the Egyptian Passover and of the exodus of the Israelites from Egypt that have their fulfillment in the final days of Jesus, His death, burial, and resurrection. This study takes you through the many details of the exodus, establishing the timeline of the events, and moves on to the New Testament where the same timeline is revealed in the events of Jesus' final days and hours. Surprisingly you will find that many of the events did not occur on the days most Christians have been told that they happened. For an exciting study get and read **Shadows of Jesus in the Exodus**.

The History of Tithing: Where Are We Today?

The doctrine of tithing 10% of one's income is taught in almost every church. Where and when did tithing begin, what was tithed upon, and to whom did it belong? Are we as new covenant believers under a command to tithe? For the complete history of tithing and whether it applies to you and me please obtain and read **The History of Tithing: Where Are We Today?**

Why Aren't Christians the Healthiest People on Earth?

It seems that most Christians believe that God exists and that He is all powerful. Most believe that He is able to heal all sicknesses and diseases, but they are not sure that He will. Some believe that He brings sickness upon us to teach us lessons. Almost everyone appears to believe that God has given us the medical system for our health and healing and many aren't sure that divine healing is happening today. **Why Aren't Christians the Healthiest People on Earth?** looks at these beliefs and more. Garry D. Pifer will share his journey in the study of divine healing, looking at what the Bible reveals. What he discovered in his study may be totally contrary to what you have been taught and have believed from childhood. This challenging and thought provoking book can be read in one or two sittings but may lead to weeks and months of study and examination on your part.

An Exposé of the Adversary

An Exposé of the Adversary looks at who the devil is, what his purpose is, where he came from, and the part he plays in our lives. **An Exposé of the Adversary** unveils and exposes the many lies he has foisted off on mankind, including the lie that Lucifer and Satan are his names. **An Exposé of the Adversary** dismantles his biggest lie, that he was an archangel that rebelled against God. Prepare to have the beliefs of a lifetime erased by **An Exposé of the Adversary.**

The Ultimate Reconciliation and Salvation of All

The Bible declares over and over again that God is unwilling for any to perish and that it is His will that all be saved. However, due to many commonly taught, and believed, doctrines of the Church most have been unable to grasp this most glorious and wonderful truth. Garry D. Pifer takes the reader through many scriptural passages showing the truth concerning these doctrines and then looks at what the Bible declares God's will and purpose to be, and the ultimate destiny of each and every individual that has ever had life. One may find what is presented challenging but also the most wonderful good news ever revealed.

DO CHRISTIANS "GO TO HEAVEN" WHEN THEY DIE?

90% of Christians believe that when they die they will go to heaven. They have heard this from infancy. Yet, if they are honest, they will have to admit that they have never heard a complete sermon or Bible study taking them from "Genesis to maps" to prove or disprove it. In **DO CHRISTIANS "GO TO HEAVEN" WHEN THEY DIE?** Garry D. Pifer will lead you in such a study and will also look at history to answer that question. You may be surprised at the answer.

These books are available from Amazon
and other major booksellers.

Made in the USA
Monee, IL
04 August 2025